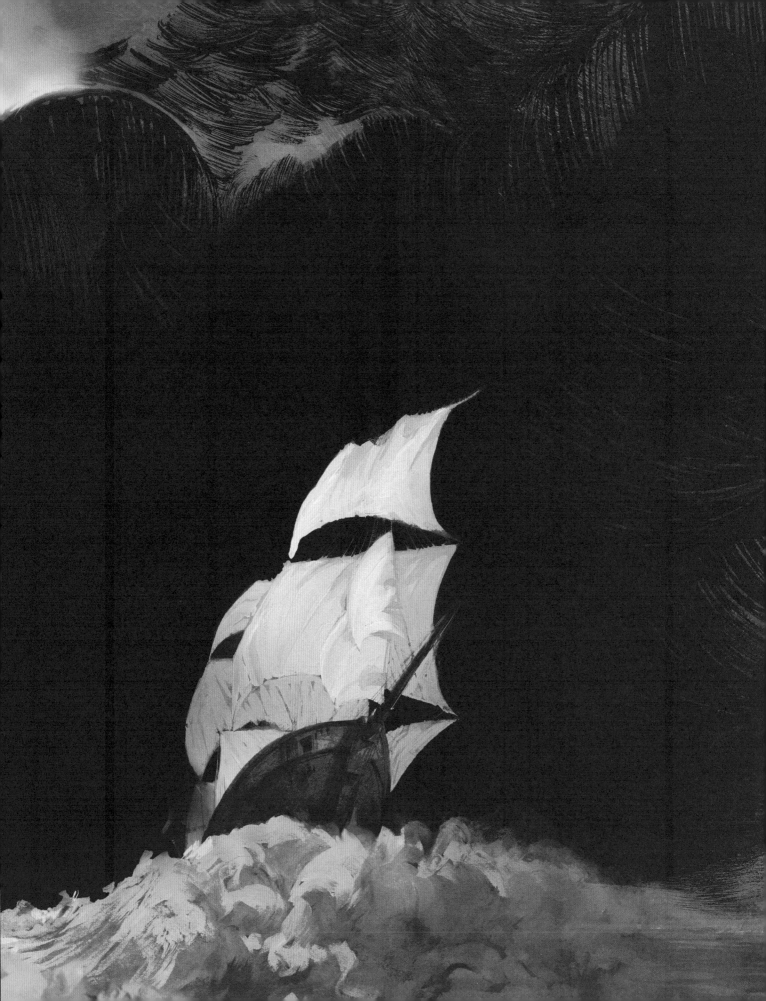

O CAPTAIN, MY CAPTAIN

WALT WHITMAN

ABRAHAM LINCOLN

AND THE CIVIL WAR

WORDS BY ROBERT BURLEIGH
ILLUSTRATIONS BY STERLING HUNDLEY

ABRAMS BOOKS FOR YOUNG READERS, NEW YORK

"I AM THE MAN, I SUFFER'D . . . . I WAS THERE."

The bearded man in the entryway softly closes the door behind him. He pauses. Standing perfectly still for a moment, he lets his eyes grow accustomed to the flickering light.

Lamps hanging from the walls cast a pale glow over a long room lined with cots, many containing a wounded soldier. The man hears the sound of breathing, the rustle of a body somewhere turning in bed.

The bare room. The gloom. The stench of sickness. Is this makeshift shed really a hospital?

Suddenly the stillness is pierced by a single sharp cry of pain. "Ohhhhhh." Is it coming from here? From over there?

The man in the doorway steps lightly across the creaking floor-boards.

The wounded soldier—so young, a boy merely—stares straight up with fixed, wide-open eyes. A stain of wet blood seeps into a crumpled bandage around one shoulder.

The man tries with careful fingers to straighten the bandage. The boy's pained, frozen gaze unlocks. He stares into the bearded face above him. "Who are you?" he seems to ask.

For a moment, the man says nothing. He holds the soldier's hand firmly in his own warm hand. Then he speaks.

"Hello. I am Walt," he says. "I am Walt Whitman."

Walt Whitman? Is this Walt Whitman, the poet?

What is a poet doing here—in the foul-smelling gloom of a Civil War hospital—among the wounded, the dying, and the dead?

One answer to that question comes from Walt Whitman himself.

"I AM LARGE . . . .
I CONTAIN MULTITUDES."

He called himself "Walt Whitman, an American, one of the roughs, a kosmos." Sometimes he was a poet. Other times he was a nurse, a comrade, or a journalist. And finally, he was mourner-in-chief for the nation's greatest president.

Could any one person be all these things, and more? Yes.

For Walt had a generous soul and a large ambition. Large enough to become America's first great poet:

> *"I celebrate myself, and sing myself,*
> *And what I assume you shall assume,*
> *For every atom belonging to me as good belongs to you."*

Large enough to praise both the tiny and the immense:

> *"I believe a leaf of grass is no less than the journeywork of the stars."*

Large enough to include all people in his vision:

> *"I am of old and young . . . I am the poet of the woman the same as the man."*

Large enough to identify with the most mistreated persons:

> *"I am the hounded slave . . . . I wince at the bite of the dogs."*

As Walt himself said, he contained multitudes—and he meant it.

"I HEAR AMERICA SINGING."

Walt Whitman loved his country. He wrote in the preface to his book of poems, *Leaves of Grass*, these unusual words: "The United States themselves are . . . the greatest poem."

And yet in the late 1850s, America's special promise—to achieve freedom and equality for all—its very democracy seemed, to Walt, dangerously at risk. For several years, he felt a dark cloud had been gathering over the land: slavery, corruption, bribery, greed, democracy scorned. Could anyone help reverse this impending storm? Walt believed so. Several years before the election of 1860, he imagined that such a person—so needed—would indeed arrive. Walt wrote that his new, hoped-for leader would be "some . . . healthy-bodied, beard-faced American." He would arrive out of "the real West and the log-hut." Walt imagined that this new president would be both "shrewd" and "heroic."

Now Northern abolitionists and industrialists faced Southern plantation and slave owners in an increasingly angry dispute about the future of the Union itself. Was there a way to resolve the crisis?

The ship was foundering and needed a captain.

And a captain did soon appear. His name?

ABRAHAM LINCOLN.

"HAVE YOU OUTSTRIPT THE REST? ARE YOU THE PRESIDENT?"

President Lincoln would say many important things to America, but the first time Walt saw him, Lincoln hardly spoke a word. In New York City in early February 1861, a humming, shuffling crowd waited for the president-elect to emerge from his hotel, the Astor House.

Standing on the roof of an omnibus near the back of the crowd, Walt Whitman watched, hoping for his first view of the man who had recently been elected, and who must now lead the nation. Walt shaded his eyes. A nearby horse stomped and snorted. There he was! Abraham Lincoln stood in the doorway, silent, looking out over the vast and murmuring ocean of faces. Walt saw everything: the tall and lanky body, the dark complexion, the "wrinkled and canny-looking" face, the all-black suit, the stovepipe hat tilted back to let a shock of black hair tumble out.

But there was something more that caught Walt's attention. It was the way Abraham Lincoln stood so confidently and firmly with hands behind his back. It was the powerful sense of certainty, the "perfect composure and coolness" that seemed to radiate from the man from Illinois.

Then, just as quickly, Lincoln stepped back inside.

Yes, Abraham Lincoln looked like the man Walt had called for. But would Lincoln be able to heal the grievous wound of slavery and keep the country together?

"BEAT! BEAT! DRUMS!—
BLOW! BUGLES! BLOW!
THROUGH THE WINDOWS—
THROUGH DOORS—
BURST LIKE A RUTHLESS FORCE."

President Abraham Lincoln did try to avert the impending war. At his first inauguration, less than a month after Walt first saw him, Lincoln said about the North and the South, "We are not enemies, but friends. Though passion may have strained, it must not break our bonds of affection." But Lincoln's words went unheard.

From Brooklyn, New York, Walt watched the ominous signs. One late evening, he was walking the New York streets after attending the opera, music still swirling in his head. Suddenly, he heard the harsh cries of newsboys hawking their papers. "War! War! War!" The headlines stood out, bold and black in the glare of the glass lanterns that lit the street. "Fort Sumter Fired On!"

It was April 12, 1861. The Civil War, the terrible conflict between the Northern states—the Union—and the Southern states—the Confederacy—had begun.

How suddenly a nation's life changes! Many people thought this war—a war that would ultimately cost more than 700,000 lives—would be over in a month. Some of the first Union troops who left New York for battle even attached ropes to their rifle barrels for the purpose of bringing back a prisoner! But just a few months later at the First Battle of Bull Run in Virginia, the once proud and optimistic Union troops were routed and chased all the way back to Washington.

And President Abraham Lincoln? He had a perfect view of this helter-skelter retreat—a disorganized array of ragged soldiers stumbling through the capital's muddy streets in disgrace—from an upper window of the White House. It became the first of many defeats, setbacks, and heartbreaks Lincoln would have to endure. "If there is a worse place than hell," he would say later, after another Union defeat with even more casualties, "I am in it."

"HE WENT HIS OWN LONELY ROAD."

From his first sighting of Abraham Lincoln, the man in the White House was never far from Walt Whitman's thoughts: "Lincoln is particularly my man . . . and by the same token, I am Lincoln's man . . . We are afloat on the same stream—we are rooted in the same ground."

What drew the poet to the president? Walt loved the fact that Lincoln, like Walt himself, came from the common people—those lacking formal education, social status, and wealth. It confirmed Walt's belief in the average person's potential for greatness.

But there was more. Both men had an almost mystical faith in the Union and in democracy. Walt's poetry arose in part from his vision of America. And much of Lincoln's political thought rested on the United States Constitution and the Declaration of Independence.

Although both men had some of the racist views of their time, and neither were ardent abolitionists, both were opposed to slavery. "If slavery is not wrong, nothing is wrong," the president once said, adding, "I cannot remember when I did not so think, and feel."

And both were poets in different ways. Lincoln's speeches, considered some of the greatest in history, were eloquent and moving, while Walt's *Leaves of Grass* was destined to become one of the world's most treasured books.

"ARM'D YEAR—YEAR OF THE STRUGGLE."

While Lincoln was making decisions that would affect hundreds of thousands, Walt anxiously observed the war from afar—his home in Brooklyn. For more than a year, he read news of the battles and saw with alarm the rising number of dead and wounded. But he did not enlist: "I could never think of myself as firing a gun or drawing a sword on another man," he once said. Still, Walt felt there was a role for him somewhere, somehow. But where? What?

Then, disturbing news arrived. Walt's brother George, who had gone off to war, was reported wounded. With no more information than that, Walt acted. He took what little money he had and set off for the battlefront.

It was a trip that would carry him much farther than he imagined.

It would carry Walt Whitman into a new life.

"DEATH IS NOTHING HERE."

Arriving at the Union Army's camp near Fredericksburg, Virginia, Walt found his brother alive and well. But wandering about the camp, Walt discovered something else: the reality of war.

What was this? He hardly dared look, but then couldn't look away.

Outside a mansion that had been turned into a hospital, a large pile of amputated legs and arms reached as high as his shoulder. On the nearby lawn, rows of blanket-covered dead soldiers lay silent in the afternoon sun. Walt lifted one of the blood-stained blankets. A face stared out without seeing—one more casualty of war.

A short distance away, on what had become the camp burial ground, small slats of wood jutted out of the earth, marking the graves. On each one of these slats was painted merely a name and a number.

Walt was struck to the core.

"I AM A FREE COMPANION . . . . I BIVOUAC BY INVADING WATCHFIRES."

But despite the suffering the Union Army had undergone (nearly 13,000 casualties in the Battle of Fredericksburg), Walt was astonished to find many of the soldiers jaunty and high-spirited. In a strange way, the tragedies they had witnessed had somehow liberated them. They had been, Walt wrote, "sifted by death." Almost immediately, he felt an intense sense of comradeship with these men.

Watching as they cooked over campfires, he shared their paltry meals, often under no roof at all. He loved their quick-witted talk, their free-and-easy slang: Hard crackers dipped in coffee were "army pies." A soldier who had gone into battle had "seen the elephant."

Sometimes, he stopped among the many wounded. What could he do? Offer a drink of water, a kind word? Yet something called him back, again and again: "I go around from one case to another. I cannot see that I do much good to these wounded and dying—but I cannot leave them."

Walt wanted to give voice to this bewildering convergence of life and death. In the moonlit darkness, he often took out his notebook and scribbled down words, lines, and even poems inspired by the scenes around him:

> "The tents of the sleeping army, the fields' and woods' dim outline,
> The darkness lit by spots of kindled fire, the silence."

After more than a week, Walt left his brother and departed from the camp. George was only slightly wounded and would continue serving throughout the war, eventually rising to the rank of lieutenant colonel (brevetted).

But Walt didn't return home to New York. Deeply affected by the soldiers he had met, he slowly felt a new purpose take root inside him. Walt Whitman's life in the hospitals of Washington—among what he would call the "great army of the sick"—was about to begin.

"I GO AROUND AMONG THESE SIGHTS . . . THE PATH I FOLLOW, I SUPPOSE I MAY SAY, IS MY OWN."

After finding lodgings in Washington, Walt—always a great walker— explored his new city. He saw crowds teeming through sometimes dusty, sometimes muddy streets. Shopkeepers, soldiers, army deserters, and runaway slaves tripped over chickens and bumped into untended cows.

And he saw more: ramshackle saloons, street peddlers, and livery stables. A canal filled with rotting, stinking garbage. And rising above everything, the unfinished dome of the Capitol Building still covered with scaffolding—a symbol of a nation divided and incomplete.

Sometimes, at night, he found himself standing in the street before the White House itself. All was quiet and dark, save for one lighted window shaded with a curtain. Was it the president's room? Did Walt see a shadow pass behind the drapery? Was Abraham Lincoln pacing back and forth?

Was the president also thinking of the dead and the dying? Was he wondering whether the threads that once held the country together would unravel past all repair? Despite recent Union losses on the battlefield, Walt knew that Lincoln had recently accomplished a very important thing. On the first day of 1863, he had signed the Emancipation Proclamation, freeing the slaves. "If I have not done anything else in my life," the president said, "I have done this."

"AMERICA, BROUGHT TO HOSPITAL IN HER FAIR YOUTH."

Walt began to learn more about the hospitals scattered throughout Washington: converted warehouses, government buildings, newly constructed sheds, large private houses—wherever enough beds could be placed. To him, the hospitals almost came to stand for the war itself: "The expression of American personality . . . is not to be looked for in the great campaign, & the battle-fights. It is to be looked for . . . in the hospitals, among the wounded."

He soon found that the wounded endured a difficult ordeal even before reaching the hospitals themselves. Often soldiers lay on the battlefield for days, untreated and uncared for, without food or much water, until a truce was called, allowing both sides to carry their wounded to their camps. And this was just the beginning.

If they survived this, what lay ahead was a painful ride down the river in an open, rough-planked barge to a wharf on the edge of Washington. But the hospitals themselves were almost as dangerous as the bloody battlegrounds. Many soldiers soon contracted diseases like dysentery, malaria, typhoid, and diarrhea (more than 75,000 died of diarrhea during the war). Those who didn't succumb had yet to suffer long hours in the hospital with too little attention, too little medicine, and too little help for the pain.

Walt was appalled at the magnitude of the suffering: "To see such things & not be able to help them is awful—I am almost ashamed of being so well & whole." As he walked through the hospital wards speaking to the soldiers and noticing his effect on them, he began to see even more clearly what his work in the war needed to be.

Walt Whitman had found a purpose beyond any he had yet experienced. Long afterward he wrote, "People used to say to me: Walt, you are doing miracles for those fellows in the hospitals. I wasn't. I was . . . doing miracles for myself."

"WHAT I GIVE I GIVE OUT OF MYSELF."

In his long poem *Song of Myself*, Walt had proclaimed, "I am the man . . . . I suffer'd . . . . I was there." Now these words would be put to the test. The sick, the wounded, the disfigured, the despairing, and the dying called out to him. And he answered.

A large, glowing, gray-bearded man (strangers would sometimes say he resembled a retired sea captain), Walt believed a friendly, magnetic personality could sometimes do as much as medicine to heal a wounded man. The smallest things mattered—how he spoke, his handshake, his smile, how he was dressed. Often he wore a necktie, and sometimes even put a flower in his buttonhole. "You can imagine," he wrote home to his mother, "I cut quite a swell." Walt wasn't picky. He took on any role he thought would help: friend, listener, assistant nurse, secretary, deliveryman, brother, father, or even mother.

His days now were much the same. Each morning, he walked to the government office where, for a small salary, he hand-copied documents until noon. Sometimes he stayed to write articles for New York newspapers about the war and hospital life: "Reader, how can I describe to you the mute appealing look that rolls and moves from many a manly eye, from many a sick cot, following you as you walk slowly down one of these wards?" He even occasionally mentioned his viewing of Lincoln passing in his carriage on the street.

Often, Walt would make afternoon hospital stops. Then returning to his small, bare room for dinner, he would eat a meagre meal (his dinner plate was simply a piece of brown paper that he crumpled and tossed into the fire after the meal was over). Before heading out again to the hospitals, he would check one of his handmade notebooks (not much of a notebook, just folded paper pinned together, sometimes stained with blood), in which he had listed the wounded soldiers' requests. He then would rifle through his supplies, stuffing gifts into a large knapsack.

Such simple needs! Bed 23: a piece of houndstooth candy. Bed 30: paper and pencil. Bed 71: an orange. Bed 77: a handful of change. Bed 98: a Bible. Taking his small store of money (he had very little and spent nearly all of it on presents for the soldiers), he might stop at a market for fruit, a stationery shop for envelopes, or a bakery for biscuits, cookies, and other sweets. Then he would walk to the hospitals.

"I SEE THE PRESIDENT
ALMOST EVERY DAY."

As Walt cared for the soldiers, he also watched Lincoln from a distance. True, Lincoln wasn't wounded. But Walt knew there are wounds that no one ever quite sees. As the war dragged on, the weary president would say to his advisers, "I must have some relief from this terrible anxiety, or it will kill me."

Lincoln received criticism for almost everything he said or did. Even his well-known habit of wordplay and joke telling was fair game for critics. But his response was a simple one: "I laugh," the president said once, "because I must not cry. That is all, that is all."

On Walt's way to the hospital in the late afternoon, he often would walk to a corner where he knew the president's carriage would pass by. Did Lincoln ever take note of this stranger who stood there watching?

Once, standing and waiting, Walt heard the sound of turning wheels and horses' hooves. The carriage carrying Abraham Lincoln slowly came into view, followed by a company of cavalry with sabers drawn and held high. Walt, his knapsack slung over his shoulder, leaned forward.

The carriage clattered past. The president looked down at Walt. Who is this? Walt Whitman gazed back at the president. Their eyes met. Abraham Lincoln seemed to nod. Walt nodded in return. Moving on, the carriage rounded a corner as Walt watched it disappear.

Simply to see this president, to catch a glimpse of his face, increasingly etched with suffering—"so awful ugly it becomes beautiful"—yet with a wry smile on occasion, was uplifting. Just to watch as the stiff figure, sitting motionless in the shadow of the carriage, passed by, gave Walt new energy. He felt Lincoln was giving his all, and beyond. How could Walt do less?

"I DO NOT ASK THE WOUNDED PERSON HOW HE FEELS . . . . I MYSELF BECOME THE WOUNDED PERSON."

Walt often found that a soldier wanted no more than to talk quietly, to hear a friendly voice, to feel a hand shake his hand, to have a pillow turned. Each soldier mattered: "Every one of these cots has its history—every case is a tragic poem, an epic, a romance, a pensive and absorbing book, if it were only written." The smallest thing made a tremendous difference. He once gave a sick and failing soldier a few pennies to buy a bottle of milk in the morning, and the soldier broke into tears of gratitude. (Later, the same soldier said that Walt's visit had saved his life.)

Walt tried to speak to each soldier in the wards he visited, attempting to give at least a word or a trifle to everyone. He read to the men—stories, poems, and newspaper articles. He played games of cards with them, or Twenty Questions. He helped them write letters home. Once he even brought ice cream—a treat many of the wounded soldiers had never tasted.

When called upon, he cleansed wounds and witnessed many amputations. (Nearly three out of four operations during the Civil War were amputations.) And always, through his long, difficult days, Walt kept his poet's eye, jotting down a few lines whenever he had a free moment. In one poem, "The Wound-Dresser," he would write:

"The hurt and wounded I pacify with soothing hand,
I sit by the restless all the dark night . . ."

Even President Lincoln surprised the wounded soldiers from time to time with an unannounced hospital visit. Deeply shaken by what he found there, he would go from bed to bed, offering an encouraging word or a friendly nod. But while these visits lifted many patients' spirits, no visit or gift could postpone the inevitable for some of the most wounded among them.

"ADIEU DEAR COMRADE, YOUR MISSION IS FULFILL'D—"

Soldiers came. And soldiers went. And many never left—alive—at all. The worst moment came too often: the deathwatch. Walt Whitman the poet had earlier written, "The smallest sprout shows there is really no death." Now Walt the nurse would sit quietly with many young soldiers as they died. Sometimes he brushed a boy's forehead with a cool cloth or held a dying soldier's hand. When the end came, there was "a pause . . . the propping pillows are removed, the limpsy head falls down, the arms are softly placed by the side . . . and the broad white sheet is thrown over everything."

But that wasn't the end of Walt's work. He would take out his little notebook, inscribe another name and address, and prepare to write a letter to the soldier's family. As he wrote to one bereaved parent, "[Your son was] one of the thousands of our unknown American young men in the ranks about whom there is no record or fame . . . but I find in them the real precious & royal ones of this land." He identified himself simply: "I am only a friend, visiting the wounded & sick soldiers."

"I SEE SO MUCH . . . SICKNESS AND SUFFERING."

Months went by. Walt's work—along with the heartbreak—was endless. Yet he was just as tireless (at war's end, he estimated he had made hundreds of hospital visits and met many thousands of soldiers).

But even Walt had his limits. As the days, weeks, and months wore on, he began to suffer spells of dizziness and occasional shortness of breath. Sometimes experiencing an illness similar to sunstroke, he began to carry an umbrella on hot, sunny days. Exhausted and anxious, his once powerful sense of well-being slowly weakened: "Days and nights of unutterable anxiety: sitting there by some poor devil destined to go: always in the presence of death."

He saw a change in Lincoln too. Over time, as he watched the president pass in the street, he noticed that Lincoln looked increasingly worn and gaunt. Others noticed it as well. The president is "the loneliest man in Washington," someone observed.

Walt remained deeply devoted to the Union. But he began to question war itself: "One's heart grows sick of war, after all, when you see what it really is . . . it seems to me like a great slaughterhouse & the men mutually butchering each other."

Walt Whitman's Civil War was beginning to take its toll.

"DEMANDS OF LIFE AND DEATH, CUT DEEPER THAN EVER UPON HIS DARK BROWN FACE."

At last, after nearly four years, the end of the war was in sight. Union troops had dealt a series of major blows to the Confederacy. William Tecumseh Sherman's army had marched through the Deep South, leaving Atlanta and the state of Georgia in ruins. At the same time, Ulysses S. Grant's army, after many terrible battles, had brought the Army of Northern Virginia, under Robert E. Lee, to the brink of surrender. It was now clear that the war would end and the Union would stand. "Thank God that I have lived to see this," Lincoln said. "It seems to me that I have been dreaming a horrid dream for four years, and now the nightmare is gone."

March 4, 1865: Lincoln's second Inauguration Day. A torrential rain had turned the Washington streets into rivers of mud, but flags still flew and cheering and applause still rang out.

Standing in the midst of the large crowd, Walt looked on. As ever, he studied Abraham Lincoln's face, noticing that the president's expression still showed "all the old goodness, tenderness, sadness, and canny shrewdness underneath the furrows."

Then something occurred that would be remarked on by many. As Lincoln began to speak, the dark clouds overhead started to part. A sudden ray of sunlight pierced the gray sky. A sign, perhaps? Lincoln would even say later: "Did you notice that sunburst? It made my heart jump."

It was one of the shortest inauguration speeches in American history. Yet it was both powerful and profound. The speech emphasized the war's destructiveness and the cause of the war—the horrific fact of slavery. At the same time, the president called for a new beginning among all those who had fought on either side: "Let us strive on to finish the work we are in; to bind up the nation's wounds; . . . to do all which may achieve and cherish a just and lasting peace, among ourselves, and with all nations."

It was almost the last time Walt Whitman would see Abraham Lincoln alive.

"O THE BLEEDING DROPS OF RED."

It was a date people at the time would remember for the rest of their lives. They would remember where they were, too, when they got the news.

April 14, 1865: President Lincoln shot. April 15, 1865: President Lincoln dead.

Walt sat in the kitchen of his mother's small, poorly furnished apartment in Brooklyn. He had come home for a short visit. Newspapers were scattered on the table in front of them. Neither Walt nor his mother had eaten, nor would they eat for the rest of the day: "We each drank half a cup of coffee; that was all."

The president was dead.

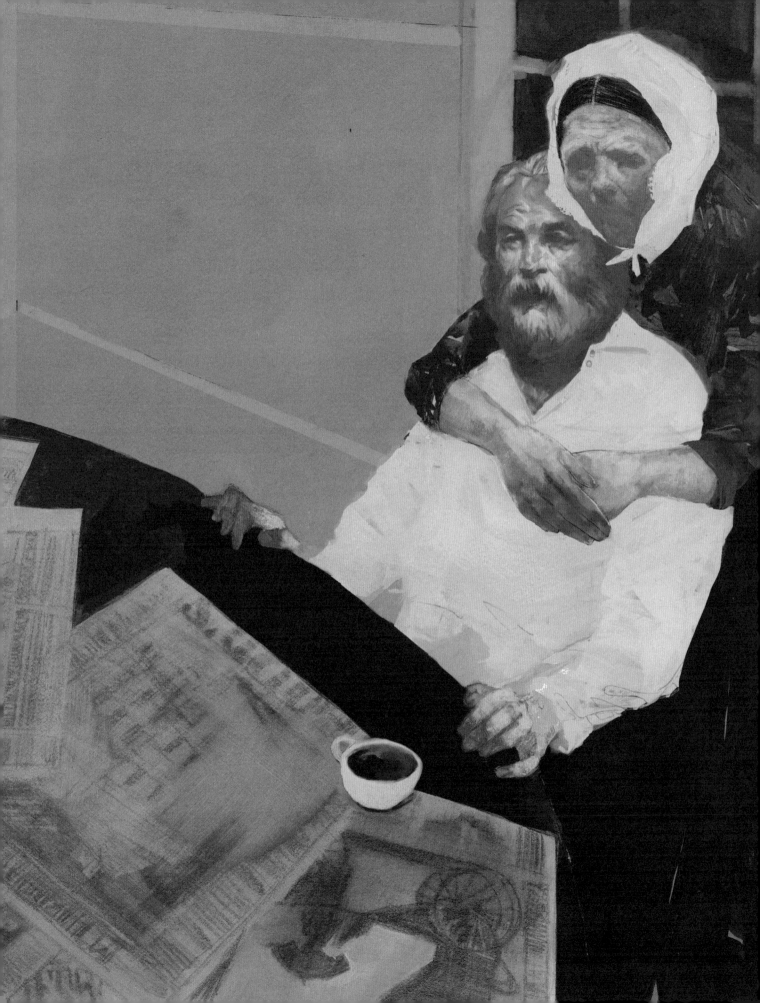

The newspapers told and retold the same story: How Lincoln and his wife were attending a play at Ford's Theatre in Washington. How the assassin, John Wilkes Booth, actor and Confederate sympathizer, mounted the stairs to the box where the Lincolns sat. How Booth pointed his gun at the president's head and pulled the trigger. How the president slumped forward as Booth leapt down to the stage, faced the astonished audience, and cried out muffled words. How Booth then fled by a side door as Mrs. Lincoln screamed, "They have shot the president!" How the president's limp body was carried to a house across the street.

How family members and friends gathered around the bed where the dying president lay. (He was so tall, his long legs hung over the bed's edge.) And finally how, as Abraham Lincoln drew his last labored breath, Secretary of War Edwin Stanton said in the quiet room: "Now he belongs to the ages."

Later that day, Walt put on his coat and went outside, into the overcast, drizzly afternoon. The Brooklyn streets were empty. Walking westward to the East River, he took the ferryboat across to Manhattan. A stillness hovered over the great city. Broadway Avenue, normally crowded with carriages and shoppers, was shut tight. Dark crepe hung in the windows of closed stores. From far off, bells tolled, and tolled again.

Walt returned home on another ferry. The gray water rose and fell against the hull of the boat. An American flag flew high above the cabin on the top deck.

And just below the flag, a large black pennant flapped and fluttered in the wind.

"O CAPTAIN! MY CAPTAIN!"

The bearded man sits at his writing table. A notebook lies open before him. In the lamplight, his memories flicker and fade: the four years of war, the battles, the hospitals, the deaths of so many soldiers he knew and loved, the assassination of Abraham Lincoln.

And what of the pain and suffering of mothers, fathers, wives, sisters, brothers, friends—the suffering of an entire nation?

His mind returns to the dead president. He seems to feel the rhythm of far-off train wheels—the slow train carrying Abraham Lincoln's body across the North to Springfield, Illinois. He knows that along that route many thousands come out to stand and watch the train as it passes—some saluting, some weeping.

Do they understand what the president endured during those horrible years? Somehow they do—that is why they come out to wait and watch—sun or rain, day or night. But perhaps they cannot put into words what they feel.

Can Walt Whitman?

The president, the man who guided the nation through the agony of a long war, is finally at rest. The captain has returned home from his awful voyage. Yes, the captain . . .

Slowly, a few words tumble onto the paper. A poem begins to take shape. Words are scratched out. New words take their place. Walt Whitman, poet, stands up, walks to the window, and stares into the darkness. He feels the poem growing in him now.

He sits again, takes up his pen, and begins to write:

"O CAPTAIN! MY CAPTAIN! OUR FEARFUL TRIP IS DONE, THE SHIP HAS WEATHER'D EVERY RACK, THE PRIZE WE SOUGHT IS WON . . ."

WALT WHITMAN
A BRIEF OVERVIEW

Walt Whitman is considered today to be one of America's greatest and most influential poets. His book of poetry, *Leaves of Grass*, is an American classic.

Born May 31, 1819, in West Hills, Long Island (near New York City), young Walt was part of a large family. His father struggled to provide for the family, and Walt was taken out of school at age 11 and sent to work.

Whitman was mostly self-educated. His various jobs during his youth and young manhood included typesetting, teaching in a one-room schoolhouse, house-building, and later working as an author and journalist. He published one novel and several short stories, none of which were particularly successful. He also worked for various newspapers in New York.

Then, in a surprising turn, he began to explore and write poetry, and in 1855 published (at his own expense) the first volume of a book that would engage him for the rest of his life, *Leaves of Grass*. The book is marked by a confident voice, a free-verse style (that is, unrhymed), and a willingness to celebrate himself and deal with various topics that were considered controversial in his time, including women's rights, sexuality, anti-slavery, and a kind of personal religion.

WALT WHITMAN, 1862. PHOTO BY MATTHEW B. BRADY. LIBRARY OF CONGRESS

During the Civil War, Whitman offered his services as an unpaid friend-nurse to thousands of wounded soldiers in Washington hospitals. Many soldiers later wrote Whitman thank-you notes and letters for helping them, and in some cases, saving their lives, in the hospitals. One or two even named a child after him!

He also strongly identified with President Abraham Lincoln. After Lincoln's death, Whitman wrote two of his most famous poems in mourning for the dead president. They are "O Captain! My Captain!" and "When Lilacs Last in the Dooryard Bloom'd."

In his later years, Whitman fell ill (due in part to his strenuous work in the hospitals), but continued to write and comment on American life and politics. He also gave lectures on the life and death of Abraham Lincoln. Walt Whitman died on March 26, 1892, and is buried in Camden, New Jersey.

ABRAHAM LINCOLN
A BRIEF OVERVIEW

Abraham Lincoln was born in a single-room log cabin on February 12, 1809, in Hardin County (now LaRue County), Kentucky. When he was a boy, the Lincoln family moved to Indiana. When Lincoln was just nine, his mother died, and for a while the boy was taken care of by his older sister, Sarah.

Lincoln had little formal education, in all probably less than one year. Yet as a youth he had a strong interest in books and learning, which he retained during his life.

After the family moved again, this time to Illinois, Lincoln—now a young man—worked at a number of jobs, such as woodcutter and shopkeeper. He also became involved in local politics. This led to his being elected to a seat in the Illinois legislature when he was just 25.

An excellent writer (for a brief time he wrote accomplished poetry), Lincoln was also a powerful public speaker. Some historians believe that he not only read an early edition of Whitman's *Leaves of Grass*, but also that he found it moving.

ABRAHAM LINCOLN, 1864. PHOTO BY MATTHEW B. BRADY. LIBRARY OF CONGRESS

He began the study of law and ran for and won a seat in the United States Congress in 1845. He served for one term before returning to Illinois and slowly becoming one of the leading lawyers in the state. Lincoln's interest in politics grew, along with his concern over the possible expansion of slavery into the western territories. He joined the newly formed Republican Party. In 1860, he ran for president of the United States and was elected, taking office on March 4, 1861.

His election led to eleven southern states seceding from the Union to form their own country, the Confederate States of America. War broke out—a war that would last four long years.

Lincoln struggled during these painful, difficult years. His many intertwined tasks were to win the war, to reunite the Union, and to end slavery (he signed the final version of the Emancipation Proclamation on January 1, 1863). In all these things he succeeded, but at a terrible price: His own health was ruined, more than 700,000 soldiers died in the war, and Lincoln himself was assassinated at the beginning of his second term as president.

Lincoln was shot (by John Wilkes Booth) the evening of April 14, 1865, while attending a play in Ford's Theatre in Washington. He died the next morning.

Lincoln's "Gettysburg Address," a short speech he gave to commemorate the Battle of Gettysburg (fought in July 1863—speech given in November), is among the most eloquent speeches delivered by any American leader. Today he is generally thought to be one of—if not *the*—greatest presidents in the history of his country.

SOME IMPORTANT DATES IN THE CIVIL WAR

November 6, 1860
Abraham Lincoln is elected president.

December 20, 1860
South Carolina becomes the first state to secede from, or leave, the United States. Ten other Southern states follow: South Carolina, Mississippi, Florida, Alabama, Georgia, Louisiana, Texas, Virginia, Arkansas, North Carolina, and Tennessee. These Southern states soon form their own country, the Confederate States of America.

March 4, 1861
Abraham Lincoln becomes president.

April 12, 1861
The Civil War begins when Confederate forces attack Fort Sumter in South Carolina.

1861–1862
Major battles fought in the first two years of the war include the First and Second Battles of Bull Run, the Battle of Shiloh, the Battle of Antietam, and the Battle of Fredericksburg.

January 1, 1863
The Emancipation Proclamation is signed.

July 1–3, 1863
The Battle of Gettysburg takes place.

September 2, 1864
Union General William Tecumseh Sherman captures the city of Atlanta, Georgia.

April 9, 1865
Confederate General Robert E. Lee surrenders to Union General Ulysses S. Grant at the Appomattox Court House in Virginia.

April 14, 1865
President Lincoln is assassinated.

TWO OF WALT WHITMAN'S "LINCOLN POEMS"

O CAPTAIN! MY CAPTAIN!

O Captain! my Captain! our fearful trip is done,
The ship has weather'd every rack, the prize we sought is won,
The port is near, the bells I hear, the people all exulting,
While follow eyes the steady keel, the vessel grim and daring;

But O heart! heart! heart!
O the bleeding drops of red,
Where on the deck my Captain lies,
Fallen cold and dead.

O Captain! my Captain! rise up and hear the bells;
Rise up—for you the flag is flung—for you the bugle trills,
For you bouquets and ribbon'd wreaths—for you the shores a-crowding,
For you they call, the swaying mass, their eager faces turning;

Here Captain! dear father!
This arm beneath your head!
It is some dream that on the deck,
You've fallen cold and dead.

My Captain does not answer, his lips are pale and still,
My father does not feel my arm, he has no pulse nor will,
The ship is anchor'd safe and sound, its voyage closed and done,
From fearful trip the victor ship comes in with object won;

Exult O shores, and ring O bells!
But I with mournful tread,
Walk the deck my Captain lies,
Fallen cold and dead.

WHEN LILACS LAST IN THE DOORYARD BLOOM'D

Long considered one of Whitman's greatest poems, this is a complex elegy
for Abraham Lincoln—one that never mentions Lincoln by name. It is built
around three symbols: the lilac flower, the hermit thrush, and the planet
Venus, which Whitman called the "western star," but we know as the "evening
star."

Here is the first section, the second section, and the concluding lines of the
poem.

I

When lilacs last in the dooryard bloom'd,
And the great star early droop'd in the western sky in the night,
I mourn'd, and yet shall mourn with ever-returning spring.

Ever-returning spring, trinity sure to me you bring,
Lilac blooming perennial and drooping star in the west,
And thought of him I love.

II

O powerful western star! O shades of night—O moody, tearful night!
O great star disappear'd—O the black murk that hides the star!
O cruel hands that hold me powerless—O helpless soul of me!
O harsh surrounding cloud that will not free my soul.

. . . .

Comrades mine and I in the midst, and their memory ever to keep, for the dead I
    loved so well,
For the sweetest, wisest soul of all my days and lands—and this for his dear sake,
Lilac and star and bird twined with the chant of my soul,
There in the fragrant pines and the cedars dusk and dim.

AUTHOR'S NOTE

I have long found it intriguing that two of America's most dramatic and heroic personalities, Abraham Lincoln and Walt Whitman, lived and worked at the same time in Washington during the Civil War years (1861–65). (The "D.C." was not added to "Washington" until 1871, when the Territory of Columbia was renamed the District of Columbia.) We have no evidence that the two men ever met, though Whitman said, and many scholars believe, they sometimes passed on the street and were in each other's presence on several other occasions.

This book is centered on Whitman's life in the capital and his work in the hospitals during those tumultuous years. Among other things, Whitman and Lincoln shared a fervent belief in the Union cause, and all through the Civil War (and after), Lincoln was never far from Whitman's mind. I should add that some vignettes were imagined to present a "you are there" feeling. But all derive from the historical facts.

I'd also like to express my appreciation for Sterling Hundley's powerful illustrations, which so beautifully bring my words to life.

One further note: All lead-in headings are quotes from Walt Whitman himself.

ARTIST'S NOTE

In one faded memory from my childhood, I'm standing in the giant outreached palm of the sculpture "The Awakening", in some corner of Washington, D.C. Grandpa and Grandma lived in Alexandria, Virginia, and on that day, they drove my brother and me to play amidst the buried aluminum giant. You can now find the enormous statue created by J. Seward Johnson, Jr., at the National Harbor in Maryland. It's odd how a 35-year-old memory seeped into the images for this story. From the start, I was searching for a device that would let me go beyond a literal interpretation of the manuscript. I wanted to draw in a touch of magic. *You see, I find sometimes fiction can be more honest than truth.*

I found an inherent conflict in the idea of Lincoln the man vs. Lincoln the myth. I played with scale to reflect Whitman's empathy for the person, as well as his consideration of our nation's commander in chief. My sketchbook is filled with unpublished notes, maps, and drawings discovered while researching Lincoln, Whitman, and Washington, D.C., during those most tumultuous years. I found *National Geographic*'s "Killing Lincoln" interactive experience to be immersive and enthralling. I had done so much research, in fact, that by the time the sketches, paintings, and ideas were well underway, I felt like I already knew the setting and source material for Spielberg's film *Lincoln*. I was able to pull from an appreciation of Civil War history—*my father is quite the expert* and has shared his knowledge and treasures as far back as I can recall. I benefited from my position as a professor at VCU in Richmond, Virginia, as the university's library offered great resources, and the city itself provided much in the way of period context and content. From these disparate sources, I tried to stitch together something credible. I tried to determine where Whitman's apartment would have been located. I sought out the correct cabin for Lincoln. I wanted to find the correct carriage, window, and vantage point—accurate information, wherever possible. I stumbled across images of Whitman's brother George, his mother and his love interest. Through my research, I was in search of those details that would pique my interest and give credibility to Burleigh's words. Yet *correct* isn't always *right*, and there are some instances when knowledge and accuracy were tweaked for the sake of artistry; for design; *for story*.

It's a careful balance, as artists are afforded this privilege to have our work read and seen by children and students. I aim to *teach facts*, but also hope to *inspire curiosity*, which can only be found where the answers are not. I trust that Burleigh and I have left enough mystery in this story to invite wandering minds to find their own answers and to seek their own paths.

ENDNOTES

Note: All Walt Whitman poem quotes are from *Leaves of Grass, The Complete 1855 and 1891–92 Editions*.

page 5. "I am the man . . . . I suffer'd . . . . I was there." Whitman, from *Leaves of Grass*, "Song of Myself," p. 64.

page 7. "I am large . . . . I contain multitudes." Whitman, from *Leaves of Grass*, "Song of Myself," p. 87.

page 7. "Walt Whitman, an American, one of the roughs, a kosmos." Whitman, from *Leaves of Grass*, "Song of Myself," p. 50.

page 7. "I celebrate myself,/ And what I assume you shall assume,/ For every atom belonging to me as good belongs to you." Whitman, from *Leaves of Grass*, "Song of Myself," p. 27.

page 7. "I believe a leaf of grass is no less than the journeywork of the stars." Whitman, from *Leaves of Grass*, "Song of Myself," p. 57.

page 7. "I am of old and young . . . I am the poet of the woman the same as the man." Whitman, from *Leaves of Grass*, "Song of Myself," p. 42, 46.

page 7. "I am the hounded slave . . . . I wince at the bite of the dogs." Whitman, from *Leaves of Grass*, "Song of Myself," p. 65.

page 8. "I hear America singing." Whitman, from *Leaves of Grass*, p. 174.

page 8. "The United States themselves are . . . the greatest poem." Whitman, from *Leaves of Grass* (Preface), p. 5.

page 9. "some . . . healthy-bodied, beard-faced American." He would arrive out of "the real West, the log-hut." Whitman, quoted in Epstein, *Lincoln and Whitman: Parallel Lives in Civil War Washington*, p. 26–27.

page 10. "Have you outstript the rest? Are you the President?" Whitman, from *Leaves of Grass*, "Song of Myself," p. 47.

page 10. "wrinkled and canny-looking" face, . . . "perfect composure and coolness" Whitman, quoted in Kaplan, *Walt Whitman: A Life*, p. 260.

page 12. "Beat! beat! drums!—blow! bugles! blow!/ Through the windows—through doors— burst like a ruthless force." Whitman, from *Leaves of Grass*, "Beat! Beat! Drums!" p. 419.

page 12. "We are not enemies, but friends. Though passion may have strained, it must not break our bonds of affection." Lincoln, quoted in McPherson, *Abraham Lincoln*, p. 30–31.

page 14. "If there is a worse place than hell, I am in it." Lincoln, quoted in Morris, *The Better Angel: Walt Whitman in the Civil War*, p. 57.

page 17. "He went his own lonely road." Whitman, quoted in Reynolds, *Walt Whitman's America: A Cultural Biography*, p. 440.

page 17. "Lincoln is particularly my man . . . and by the same token, I am Lincoln's man . . . We are afloat on the same stream—we are rooted in the same ground." Whitman, quoted in Epstein, *Lincoln and Whitman: Parallel Lives in Civil War Washington*, p. 90.

page 17. "If slavery is not wrong, nothing is wrong. I cannot remember when I did not so think, and feel." Lincoln, quoted in Leidner, *Abraham Lincoln: Quotes, Quips, and Speeches*, p. 64.

page 18. "Arm'd year—year of the struggle." Whitman, from *Leaves of Grass*, "Eighteen Sixty-One," p. 418.

page 18. "I could never think of myself as firing a gun or drawing a sword on another man." Whitman, quoted in Kaplan, *Walt Whitman: A Life*, p. 262.

page 18. "Death is nothing here." Whitman, quoted in Callow, *From Noon to Starry Night: A Life of Walt Whitman*, p. 288.

page 20. "I am a free companion . . . . I bivouac by invading watchfires." Whitman, from *Leaves of Grass*, "Song of Myself" p. 64.

page 20. "sifted by death." Morris, *The Better Angel: Walt Whitman in the Civil War*, p. 69.

page 20. "army pies." "seen the elephant." Morris, *The Better Angel: Walt Whitman in the Civil War*, p. 51, 55.

page 20. "I go around from one case to another. I do not see that I do much good to these wounded and dying—but I cannot leave them." Whitman, quoted in Callow, *From Noon to Starry Night: A Life of Walt Whitman*, p. 290.

page 20. "The tents of the sleeping army, the fields' and woods' dim outline,/The darkness lit by spots of kindled fire, the silence." Whitman, from *Leaves of Grass*,

"By the Bivouac's Fitful Flame," p. 436.

page 20. "great army of the sick" Whitman, quoted in Callow, *From Noon to Starry Night: A Life of Walt Whitman*, p. 294.

page 22. "I go around among these sights . . . the path I follow, I suppose I may say, is my own." Whitman, quoted in Price, "Whitman's *Drum Taps* and Washington's Civil War Hospitals," http://xroads.virginia.edu/~CAP/hospital/whitman.htm.

page 22. "If I have not done anything else in my life, I have done this." Lincoln, quoted in Handlin and Handlin, *Abraham Lincoln and the Union*, p. 159.

page 24. "America, brought to Hospital in her fair youth." Whitman, quoted in Kaplan, *Walt Whitman: A Life*, p. 277.

page 24. "The expression of American personality . . . is not to be looked for in the great campaign, & the battle-fights. It is to be looked for . . . in the hospitals, among the wounded." Whitman, quoted in Price, "Whitman's *Drum Taps* and Washington's Civil War Hospitals," http://xroads.virginia.edu/~CAP/hospital/whitman.htm.

page 24. "To see such things & not be able to help them is awful—I feel almost ashamed of being so well & whole." Whitman, quoted in Morris, *The Better Angel: Walt Whitman in the Civil War*, p. 119.

page 24. "People used to say to me: Walt, you're doing miracles for those fellows in the hospitals. I wasn't. I was . . . doing miracles for myself." Whitman, quoted in Morris, *The Better Angel: Walt Whitman in the Civil War*, p. 100.

page 27. "What I give I give out of myself." Whitman, from *Leaves of Grass*, "Song of Myself," p. 72.

page 27. "You can imagine, I cut quite a swell." Whitman, quoted in Kaplan, *Walt Whitman: A Life*, p. 280.

page 29. "Reader, how can I describe to you the mute appealing look that rolls and moves from many a manly eye, from many a sick cot, following you as you walk slowly down one of these wards?" Whitman, quoted in Morris, *The Better Angel: Walt Whitman in the Civil War*, p. 107.

page 30. "I see the president almost every day." Whitman, quoted in Epstein, *Lincoln and Whitman: Parallel Lives in Civil War Washington*, p.172.

page 30. "I must have some relief from this terrible anxiety or it will kill me." Lincoln, quoted in Epstein,

Lincoln and Whitman: Parallel Lives in Civil War Washington, p. 219.

page 30. "I laugh because I must not cry. That is all, that is all." Lincoln, quoted in Epstein, *Lincoln and Whitman: Parallel Lives in Civil War Washington*, p. 359.

page 30. "so awful ugly it becomes beautiful" Whitman, quoted in Kaplan, *Walt Whitman: A Life*, p. 271.

page 32. "I do not ask the wounded person how he feels . . . . I myself become the wounded person." Whitman, from *Leaves of Grass*, p. 65.

page 32. "Every one of these cots has its history—every case is a tragic poem, an epic, a romance, a pensive and absorbing book, if it were only written." Whitman, quoted in Price, "Whitman's *Drum Taps* and Washington's Civil War Hospitals," http://xroads.virginia.edu/~CAP/hospital/whitman.htm.

page 32. "The hurt and wounded I pacify with soothing hand, /I sit by the restless all the dark night." Whitman, from *Leaves of Grass*, "The Wound-Dresser," p. 445.

page 34. "Adieu, dear comrade, Your mission is fulfill'd—" Whitman, from *Leaves of Grass*, "Adieu to a Soldier," p. 457.

page 34. "The smallest sprout shows there is really no death." Whitman, from *Leaves of Grass*, p. 32.

page 34. "a pause . . . the propping pillows are removed, the limpsy head falls down, the arms are softly placed by the side . . . and the broad white sheet is thrown over everything." Whitman, quoted in Morris, *The Better Angel: Walt Whitman in the Civil War*, p. 143.

page 34. "[Your son was] one of the thousands of our unknown American men in the ranks about whom there is no record or fame—but I find in them the real precious & royal ones of this land." Whitman, quoted in Morris, *The Better Angel: Walt Whitman in the Civil War*, p. 130.

page 34. "I am only a friend, visiting the wounded & sick soldiers." Whitman, quoted in Morris, *The Better Angel: Walt Whitman in the Civil War*, p. 128.

page 36. "I see so much . . . sickness and suffering." Whitman, quoted in Epstein, *Lincoln and Whitman: Parallel Lives in Civil War Washington*, p. 171.

page 36. "Days and nights of unutterable anxiety: sitting there by some poor devil destined to go: always in the presence of death." Whitman, quoted in Epstein, *Lincoln and Whitman: Parallel Lives in Civil War Washington*, p. 244.

page 36. "the loneliest man in Washington." Epstein, *Lincoln and Whitman: Parallel Lives in Civil War Washington*, p. 117.

page 36. "One's heart grows sick of war after all, when you see what it really is . . . it seems to me like a great slaughter-house & the men mutually butchering each other." Whitman, quoted in Epstein, *Lincoln and Whitman: Parallel Lives in Civil War Washington*, p. 169.

page 38. "demands of life and death cut deeper than ever upon his dark brown face." Whitman, Walt. *Prose Works*, "I. Specimen Days; 77. The Inauguration," Philadelphia: David McCay, 1892; Bartleby.com, 2000. www.bartleby.com/229/

page 38. "Thank God I have lived to see this. It seems to me that I have been dreaming a horrid dream for four years, and now the nightmare is gone." McPherson, *Abraham Lincoln*. p. 59–60.

page 41. "all the old goodness, tenderness, sadness, and canny shrewdness underneath the furrows." Whitman, quoted in Morris, *The Better Angel: Walt Whitman in the Civil War*, p. 206.

page 41. "Did you notice that sunburst? It made my heart jump." Lincoln, quoted in Roper, *Now the Drum of War: Walt Whitman and His Brothers in the Civil War*, p. 335.

page 41. "Let us strive on to finish the work we are in; to bind up the nation's wounds; . . . to do all which may achieve and cherish a just and lasting peace, among ourselves, and with all nations." Lincoln, quoted in Leidner, *Abraham Lincoln: Quotes, Quips, and Speeches*, p. 136.

page 42. "O the bleeding drops of red." Whitman, from *Leaves of Grass* "O Captain! My Captain!" p. 467.

page 42. "We each drank half a cup of coffee; that was all." Whitman, quoted in Callow, *From Noon to Starry Night: A Life of Walt Whitman*, p. 317.

page 44. "They have shot the president!" Mary Todd Lincoln, quoted in Donald, *Lincoln*, p. 597.

page 46. "Now he belongs to the ages." Secretary of War Stanton, quoted in Donald, *Lincoln*, p. 599.

page 49. "O Captain! My Captain!" Whitman, from *Leaves of Grass* "O Captain! My Captain!" p. 467.

page 50. "O Captain! my Captain! our fearful trip is done, /The ship has weather'd every rack, the prize we sought is won." Whitman, from *Leaves of Grass* "O Captain! My Captain!" p. 467.

BIBLIOGRAPHY

Callow, Philip. *From Noon to Starry Night: A Life of Walt Whitman*. Chicago: Ivan R. Dee, 1992.

Donald, David Herbert. *Lincoln*. New York: Simon & Schuster, 1995.

Dutton, Geoffrey. *Whitman*. New York: Grove Press, Inc., 1961.

Epstein, Daniel Mark. *Lincoln and Whitman: Parallel Lives in Civil War Washington*. New York: Random House, 2005.

Freedman, Russell. *Lincoln: A Photobiography*. New York: Houghton Mifflin Company, 1987.

Handlin, Oscar and Lilian Handlin. *Abraham Lincoln and the Union*. Boston, Toronto: Little, Brown and Company, 1980.

Holzer, Harold, ed. *Lincoln As I Knew Him*. New York: Workman Publishing, 1999.

Kaplan, Justin. *Walt Whitman: A Life*. New York: Simon & Schuster, 1980.

Leidner, Gordon. *Abraham Lincoln: Quotes, Quips, and Speeches*. Nashville, Tennessee: Cumberland House Publishing, 2009.

McPherson, James M. *Abraham Lincoln*. New York: Oxford University Press, 2009.

Morris, Roy, Jr. *The Better Angel: Walt Whitman in the Civil War*. New York: Oxford University Press, 2000.

Oates, Stephen B. *Abraham Lincoln: The Man Behind the Myths*. New York: Harper and Row, 1984.

Price, Angel. "Whitman's *Drum Taps* and Washington's Civil War Hospitals." http://xroads.virginia.edu/~CAP/hospital/whitman.htm.

Reef, Catherine. *Walt Whitman*. New York: Clarion Books, a Houghton Mifflin imprint, 1995.

Reynolds, David S. *Walt Whitman's America: A Cultural Biography*. New York: Alfred A. Knopf, Inc., 1995.

Roper, Robert. *Now the Drum of War: Walt Whitman and His Brothers in the Civil War*. New York: Walker & Company, 2008.

Sandburg, Carl. *Abraham Lincoln*. New York: Charles Scribner's Sons, 1939.

Schmidgall, Gary. *Walt Whitman: A Gay Life*. New York: Penguin Publishing Group, 1997.

Sinha, Manisha. "Allies for Emancipation? Lincoln and Black Abolitionists," from *Our Lincoln*. Edited by Eric Foner. New York: W. W. Norton, 2008.

Whitman, Walt. *Leaves of Grass: The Complete 1855 and 1891–92 Editions*. New York: First Library of America Paperback Classic Edition, 2011.

Whitman, Walt. *Prose Works*, "I. Specimen Days; 77. The Inauguration," Philadelphia: David McCay, 1892; Bartleby.com, 2000. www.bartleby.com/229/

Whitman, Walt, Roy P. Basler, ed. *Memoranda During the War and Death of Abraham Lincoln*. Bloomington, Indiana: Indiana University Press, 1962.

Whitman, Walt, Richard M. Bucke, ed. *The Wound Dresser*. New York: The Bodley Press, 1949.

Whitman, Walt, Walter Lowenfels, ed. *Walt Whitman's Civil War*. New York: Alfred A. Knopf, Inc., 1960.

Zweig, Paul. *Walt Whitman: The Making of the Poet*. New York: Basic Books, 1984.

INDEX

NOTE: PAGE NUMBERS IN *ITALICS* REFER TO ILLUSTRATIONS.

assassination, Lincoln, 42, 44, 44–46, 46,
    54–55

Booth, John Wilkes, 44

Civil War
    beginning of, 13, *13*, 55
    deaths, 14, 54
    end of, 38
    Lincoln inauguration speech on, 12, *12*
    major battles of, 14, 55
    Whitman impressions of, 18, *18–19*, 49
Confederacy, 13, 38, 54, 55

democracy, 8, 17

election (1860), 8–9, 54, 55
Emancipation Proclamation, 22, 54, 55

First Battle of Bull Run, 14, 55
Ford's Theatre, 44, *45*, 55
Fort Sumter, 13, *13*, 55
Fredericksburg, Virginia, 18, 55

"Gettysburg Address" (Lincoln), 55
Grant, Ulysses S., 38, 55

hospitals
    Whitman impressions of, 24, 29
    Whitman working in, *4–5*, 5, 29, 53

inauguration speeches, 12, *12*, 38, *38–40*, 41

Leaves of Grass (Whitman), 8, 17, 53, 54
Lee, Robert E., 38, 55

New York City
    Lincoln in, 10, 11
    Whitman working in, 53
Nurse Whitman
    hospital work by, *4–5*, 5, 29, 53
    interactions with soldiers, 29, 32, 33, 34,
        35

"O Captain! My Captain!" (Whitman), 50,
    53, 56

poems, 7
    Leaves of Grass book of, 8, 17, 53, 54
    "O Captain! My Captain!," 50, 53, 56
    "Song of Myself," 27
    "When Lilacs Last in the Dooryard
        Bloom'd," 53, 57
    "The Wound-Dresser," 32

Sherman, William Tecumseh, 38, 55
slavery, 10
    dispute over, 8–9
    Emancipation Proclamation and, 22, 55
    Lincoln on, 17
soldiers, 53
    in hospital, *4–5*, 5
    Lincoln visiting, 32
    Whitman impressions of, 20, *21*, 24
    Whitman interactions with, 29, 32, *33*,
        34, 35
"Song of Myself" (Whitman), 27
Stanton, Edwin, 46
suffering, 24
    of Lincoln, 30, 31, 36, 37
    of Whitman, 36

Union Army, 13, 14, 18, 38, 55

Washington
    Ford's Theatre in, 44, *45*, 55
    hospitals in, 24, 53
    Whitman impressions of, 22, 23
"When Lilacs Last in the Dooryard Bloom'd"
    (Whitman), 53, 57
"The Wound-Dresser" (Whitman), 32